Norman Normal:
Day of the Gnomes

Level 11 – Lime

BookLife

Helpful Hints for Reading at Home

The focus phonemes (units of sound) used throughout this series are in line with the order in which your child is taught at school. This offers a consistent approach to learning whether reading at home or in the classroom.

HERE ARE SOME COMMON WORDS THAT YOUR CHILD MIGHT FIND TRICKY:

water	where	would	know	thought	through	couldn't
laughed	eyes	once	we're	school	can't	our

TOP TIPS FOR HELPING YOUR CHILD TO READ:

- Encourage your child to read aloud as well as silently to themselves.
- Allow your child time to absorb the text and make comments.
- Ask simple questions about the text to assess understanding.
- Encourage your child to clarify the meaning of new vocabulary.

This book focuses on developing independence, fluency and comprehension. It is a lime level 11 book band.

CAMBRIDGESHIRE LIBRARIES	
10010010596587	
Askews & Holts	12-Apr-2021
JF Yellow-FS	

Norman Normal: Day of the Gnomes

Written by Robin Twiddy

Illustrated by Kris Jones

Chapter One
Not a Normal Day

Norman was a normal eight-year-old boy. He did normal things. In fact, even his name was normal. Norman Normal. Every Saturday morning, his mum would drag him around the garden centre. It was so boring. But it was on one of those boring mornings in the garden centre that Norman Normal's life became anything but normal.

Norman was distracted, thinking about all the better things he could be doing on a Saturday morning, when he bumped into a display of garden gnomes. One of the gnomes wobbled on the edge of the table, then fell to the floor with a crash. That was when the strangeness began.

The plastic gnome cracked open and out crawled a little man. No, it wasn't a little man but a real gnome! Norman was shocked – he didn't know what to do.

"Hello, my name is Norman. Sorry, I knocked you over. Are you okay?"

The gnome stood up and stretched his arms. "Ah, that's better," said the gnome. He looked Norman up and down. "Quickly Norbin…" he said.

"Um, actually it's Norman," said Norman.

"Norman," said the gnome, "quickly, put me in your bag."

Norman opened his bag and the gnome hopped in.

Chapter Two

There's Gnome Place like Home

When Norman got home, he ran to his bedroom, slammed the door and opened his bag. Was it real? Did he really have a gnome in his backpack?

"You can come out now. It's safe," Norman said.

The gnome crawled out of Norman's bag and stood on his bed. "Hello, Norman, I am Knots the Gnome," said Knots, with a little bow.

"What were you doing in the garden centre, Knots?" asked Norman.

Knots explained that he had been captured by two humans who had dipped him in plastic and sold him to the garden centre.

"I don't think I am the only one," Knots said.

"Yeah," interrupted Norman. "I saw loads of gnomes in the garden centre, more than I have ever seen before."

"Well this isn't good," said Knots. "Gnomes are very important! Without gnomes, things are going to start going very wrong for you humans."

Knots explained that gnomes are the invisible helpers of the human world. They do all the things that people forget to do, and people are more forgetful than you would think. Gnomes plug in your tablets and phones at night, they feed your cat when you forget, and tie your shoelaces for you when you are not looking.

"That's what I am good at," said Knots, "tying and untying knots. That's how I got my name. We gnomes are named after what we are good at. You should meet my friend Nose Picker; do you want to know what he is good at?"

"No," said Norman very quickly.

Knots asked Norman to help him stop the gnome hunters. Norman agreed to help Knots, but he didn't really know how to find gnome hunters or what to do when he did.

Norman found a wooden toy castle.

"Here, Knots, you can stay in this castle until we find the gnome hunters," he said.

Chapter Three

Gnome Help

It wasn't long before Norman noticed the bright side of living with a gnome. His tablet never ran out of battery anymore, he didn't trip over untied shoelaces and his bike chain was always greased. But more than that, Knots was really fun.

That week, Norman and Knots had lots of fun and became good friends. But soon it was Saturday again, and Norman knew what that meant… a trip to the garden centre. When he told Knots, the gnome looked very worried. "Do you think the gnome hunters will be there?" asked Knots.

"I don't know," Norman said. "If they are, what will we do?"
Knots paused. "I don't know," he said.
Norman felt nervous, but he had promised to help save the other gnomes.
"Don't worry, we will find them and stop them," Norman said, feeling less sure than he sounded.

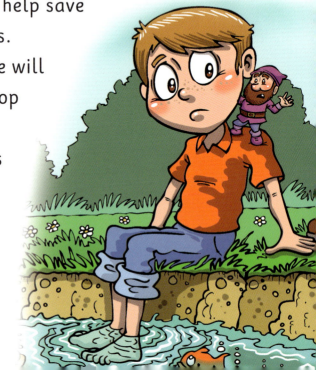

Chapter Four

Mr Chunk

Saturday morning came and Norman found himself at the garden centre again with his mum. But this time, Knots was there too.
"Oh, look, a sale on plastic flowers. Norman, you stay here and look at the flowerpots," said Mum as she walked away.
This was Norman's chance to investigate.

As soon as Norman's mum was out of sight, Knots appeared on Norman's shoulder.
"Do you know what the gnome hunters look like?" asked Norman.
"I only saw them for a moment," said Knots, thinking hard. "One was tall and thin, and the other one was short and fat, and they both smelled really bad!"
Norman and Knots snuck away in search of clues.

They had been searching for ages when Knots stopped.

"Listen! I think that's one of them."

Norman stopped to listen. Voices were coming from the other side of some big potted plants. Norman climbed into the tangle of leaves to see if he could see the men.

Norman pulled a leaf aside and peered through. In front of him was a short, round man wearing a sleeveless leather jacket and a flat cap, with what looked like yesterday's dinner all down his front. He was talking with the manager of the garden centre.

"I told you, we've got fifty more in the van if you want them," said the fat man.
"Well, Mr Chunk, your gnomes have been selling like hotcakes. How do you make them so realistic?" asked the manager.
"Trade secret," said Chunk, with a sly smile.

Chapter Five

Gnome Delivery

Norman followed Chunk and the manager out to the carpark. There he saw them walk up to a van with 'Flake and Chunk's Gnome and Flamingo Garden Accessories' written on the side.

"Did you ever wonder why you never see any real flamingos around Chatsworth?" Knots asked, pointing at the van. "They got them too!"

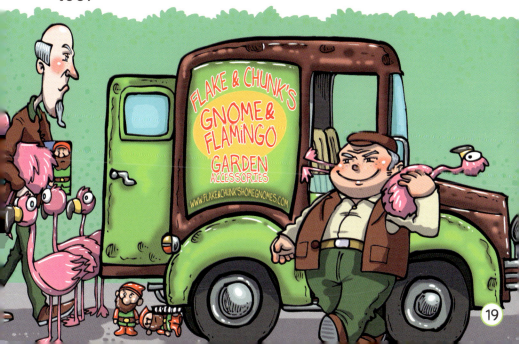

A tall, skinny man climbed out of the van and shook hands with the manager.

"That must be Flake," thought Norman.

"Just around here," said Flake, in a squeaky voice.

When he swung open the doors on the van, Norman and Knots saw that it was full of gnomes and bright pink flamingos.

"Excellent," said the manager. "I will take the lot. Bring them in."

"We are almost out of gnomes," said Flake when the manager had left.

"Well, we will just have to catch some more," replied Chunk.

Norman quickly took a picture of the two men and their van.

Chapter Six

Now we Gnome

When they got home, Norman ran to the computer and looked at the pictures of the van.
"There!" said Norman, pointing at the website address on the side of the van. He punched it into the computer and a picture of Flake and Chunk popped up on the screen.

Norman explored the website until he found what he was looking for: their address.
"That's just around the corner from here," Norman said. "I pass it every day on the way to school. On Monday morning, we will leave early and see if we can find out anything about Flake and Chunk."

Chapter Seven

What the Gnome Saw

On Monday morning, Norman and Knots left early for school. When they reached the address, Norman saw what he was looking for. "That must be the place," said Norman, pointing out a mouldy-looking building. "Look, there's a window. Hold me up so I can see," Knots said.

Norman held Knots up to a window. Knots cleaned some grime off the glass and peered into the gnome factory. Inside, Knots could see Flake and Chunk hard at work. Knots didn't want to, but he made himself keep watching.

The tall, skinny man was forcing a gnome to hold a fishing rod. Then the round, short man grabbed the gnome and dipped him into a barrel of plastic. The poor gnome didn't even know what had happened.

Chunk started painting the gnome. "Flake?" he said, still concentrating on the gnome.
"Yes, Chunk?"
"Have you found any new gnome homes?" asked Chunk.
"As a matter of fact, I have. I will get the gnome-catching gear together and we will go hunting tomorrow night," Flake said, stroking his thin, greasy beard.

Knots had seen enough. "Bring me down, Norman," said Knots. When they were finally eye to eye – Knots was stood on a dustbin – the gnome said, "I have a plan, but we are going to need some help."

Chapter Eight
The Big Plan

Knots explained his plan to Norman on the journey to school. They had a lot of work to do. Norman thought that he should be scared, or at least worried. After all, this wasn't normal, and everything about Norman was normal – even his name. But he was actually excited.

After school, Knots and Norman wrote an email to Flake and Chunk. It read:
Dear Mr Flake and Mr Chunk. My name is Mr Megabucks and I make free television adverts for companies that I really like. If you would like a free advert, please meet me at your gnome factory at 7 o'clock this evening.
P.S. Dress like gnomes. Yours sincerely, Mr Megabucks.

With that part of the plan taken care of, Norman told his mum he was going out to play on his bike. Norman and Knots sped around the neighbourhood and every time they saw a gnome in a garden, Norman would smash it and Knots would tell the gnome to go to Norman's house.

Norman knew that he would be in trouble if he was caught, and he didn't like breaking other people's property, even though it was to help the gnomes.
Before long, Norman had lost track of how many gnomes they had freed. It was time to go home.

When Norman got home, he brushed his teeth, said goodnight to his mum and went up to his room. When Norman walked into his bedroom, nearly one hundred gnomes cheered, "Norman, champion of the gnomes!"
"Shhhhhh," said Norman, looking panicked. "My mum is downstairs!"

Chapter Nine

The Day of the Gnomes

When Norman arrived at the gnome factory the next evening with his army of gnomes, he was feeling very nervous.

"I have to do this for Knots. He's my best friend," Norman thought.

"Right, lads," Knots said to the gathered gnomes. "You all know what you need to do."

The gnomes disappeared into the factory through drainpipes, open windows and air vents. Norman put on his disguise and headed to the front door. His disguise was made up of his dad's old overcoat, a brimmed hat, dark glasses and a moustache made from glue and the bristles of an old paintbrush.

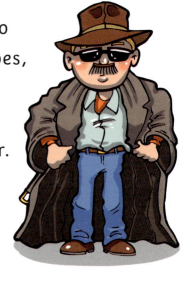

Norman knocked on the door of the factory. The door opened to reveal one very tall, skinny gnome and one short and very round gnome. Flake and Chunk had done just what the email had asked. They were wearing pointed hats, long grey beards and boots.

"Mr Megabucks?" the shorter of the two giant gnomes asked. "You are a little shorter than I expected. Come in."
"We are looking forward to making our first television advert," said Flake. "Where are the cameras?"
"They will be here very soon," Norman said in the deepest voice he could manage.

As Norman walked over to the work area, with the big barrels of liquid plastic, the paints and little fishing rods, Flake whispered into Chunk's ear, "Isn't he a bit short to be a millionaire?"
"Maybe he grew up in a house with really low ceilings," replied Chunk.

Although Norman had Chunk fooled, Flake seemed to be suspicious. "I think we should shoot the advert over here near the workbenches. What do you think, Mr Chunk?" Norman said in his best Mr Megabucks voice. Before Chunk could answer Flake interrupted, "Mr Megabucks, I looked you up online, and nobody has ever heard of you."

With that, Flake knocked off Norman's hat and yanked at his moustache until it came loose. "I knew it! He's just a boy!" screamed Flake in his high-pitched voice.

"Well what are we going to do with you then?" said Chunk, picking up a length of rope. Chunk and Flake loomed over Norman.

"Hey, if we aren't making an advert anymore, we can go gnome hunting," said Flake, excitedly. Flake and Chunk tied Norman up. You would have thought that Norman would be worried, but he wasn't. Everything was going according to plan.

They put Norman into a backroom of the factory and went off to get their gnome-catching gear. As soon as Flake and Chunk were out of sight, Knots appeared.
"Never fear," Knots said. "Knots are my speciality." Within seconds Norman was free.
"Are the others in position?" Norman asked.

"They sure are," said Knots. The two friends headed out of the backroom into a maze of shelves. The shelves were full of gnomes, pink flamingos, pots of paint and all sorts of dusty and dirty things.
"Here comes the fun part," said Knots to Norman.

Flake and Chunk didn't notice all the extra gnomes on the shelves. They probably should have, but they didn't. They were still angry about the advert. But Chunk did notice the tin of paint that hit him on the back of the head.

"Ouch! What's going on?" shouted Chunk.
"Who's there?" shouted Flake, looking around. "Come out!"
"You have been naughty boys, haven't you?" came a little voice from up ahead of the pair. It was followed by laughter from all directions.

"I'm scared," Chunk said, hugging his partner tight.

"Me too," said Flake, shaking a little.
There was a crash behind them, and the two men jumped. It was a plastic flamingo thrown by a gnome named Clapper. The flamingo cracked open like an egg and a great big pink flamingo flew up into the air.

Now Chunk noticed the gnomes on the shelves. They were all holding pink flamingos like spears. "Quick, run!" shouted Chunk and the pair started running as fast as they could. As they ran, they could hear a 'CRASH, CRASH, CRASH' behind them as more and more flamingos broke free and filled the air.

Flake and Chunk couldn't see anything for flamingos. The air was full of them. Then they heard Norman's voice. "You should have left the gnomes alone. Now you have to deal with me, Norman Normal!"

"This is all your fault!" screamed Flake. His high-pitched voice was almost lost among the squawks of the flamingos.

The two villains leapt towards Norman's voice, but something was wrong. Their shoelaces were tied together. "Knots did his bit!" thought Norman, as he ducked to the side. The two fully grown men, dressed as gnomes, tumbled past him and landed in the barrels of liquid plastic.

Once the plastic had set, the gnomes started painting Flake and Chunk. Before Norman knew what had happened, the two gnome hunters looked like two very large garden gnomes.

"I don't think those two are going to be bothering you all for a while," Norman said to the gnomes. They all cheered, "Norman, champion of the gnomes!"

Chapter Ten
Never Normal Again

The next day the garden centre manager was surprised to see two people-sized gnomes waiting for him in the carpark with a note that read: 'Dear Mr Manager, thank you for buying all our gnomes. We have gone out of business. Please accept these two giant gnomes as a gift. Yours, Flake and Chunk.'
The manager was also surprised by all the pink flamingos.

Norman's life went back to normal after that day. Well, almost normal. He now had lots of little friends and his town was full of pink flamingos. Norman didn't mind going to the garden centre anymore, because there were two giant gnomes there that reminded him of the day he saved the gnomes.

Norman Normal: Day of the Gnomes

1. How did Knots get his name?

2. What sale items did Norman's mum go and look at?
   (a) Flowerpots
   (b) Plastic flowers
   (c) Gnomes

3. How did the army of gnomes get into the factory?

4. What was the name of the gnome that threw the first flamingo on the floor?

5. Why do you think Norman would have been in trouble if he had been caught smashing the gnomes? Do you think it was the right thing to do?

©This edition published 2021.
First published in 2020.
BookLife Publishing Ltd.
King's Lynn, Norfolk PE30 4LS

ISBN 978-1-83927-024-6

All rights reserved. Printed in Malta.
A catalogue record for this book is available from the British Library.

Norman Normal: Day of the Gnomes
Written by Robin Twiddy
Illustrated by Kris Jones

An Introduction to BookLife Readers...

Our Readers have been specifically created in line with the London Institute of Education's approach to book banding and are phonetically decodable and ordered to support each phase of the Letters and Sounds document.

Each book has been created to provide the best possible reading and learning experience. Our aim is to share our love of books with children, providing both emerging readers and prolific page-turners with beautiful books that are guaranteed to provoke interest and learning, regardless of ability.

BOOK BAND GRADED using the Institute of Education's approach to levelling.

PHONETICALLY DECODABLE supporting each phase of Letters and Sounds.

EXERCISES AND QUESTIONS to offer reinforcement and to ascertain comprehension.

BEAUTIFULLY ILLUSTRATED to inspire and provoke engagement, providing a variety of styles for the reader to enjoy whilst reading through the series.

**AUTHOR INSIGHT:
ROBIN TWIDDY**

Robin Twiddy is one of BookLife Publishing's most creative and prolific editorial talents, who imbues all his copy with a sense of adventure and energy. Robin's Cambridge-based first class honours degree in psychosocial studies offers a unique viewpoint on factual information and allows him to relay information in a manner that readers of any age are guaranteed to retain. He also holds a certificate in Teaching in the Lifelong Sector, and a postgraduate certificate in Consumer Psychology.

A father of two, Robin has written over 70 titles for BookLife and specialises in conceptual, role-playing narratives which promote interaction with the reader and inspire even the most reluctant of readers to fully engage with his books.

This book focuses on developing independence, fluency and comprehension. It is a lime level 11 book band.